handshake
by Claire Albrecht

PUNCHER & WATTMANN

First published in 2022

Published by Puncher and Wattmann
PO Box 279
Waratah NSW 2298

www.puncherandwattmann.com
poetry@puncherandwattmann.com

A catalogue record for this
work is available from the
National Library of Australia

ISBN 9781922571328

Cover design by Claire Albrecht
Printed by Lightning Source International

Only truthful hands write truthful poems.
PAUL CELAN

And I am not exactly a crying person, though my eyes
tear up frequently because of my allergies.
CLAUDIA RANKINE

gannet

you discover my weaknesses with a gannet's precision dive

and a somersault pike. huh, what a fragility,

like a rushed nest of sticks

precarious on a

cliff fa

ce

.

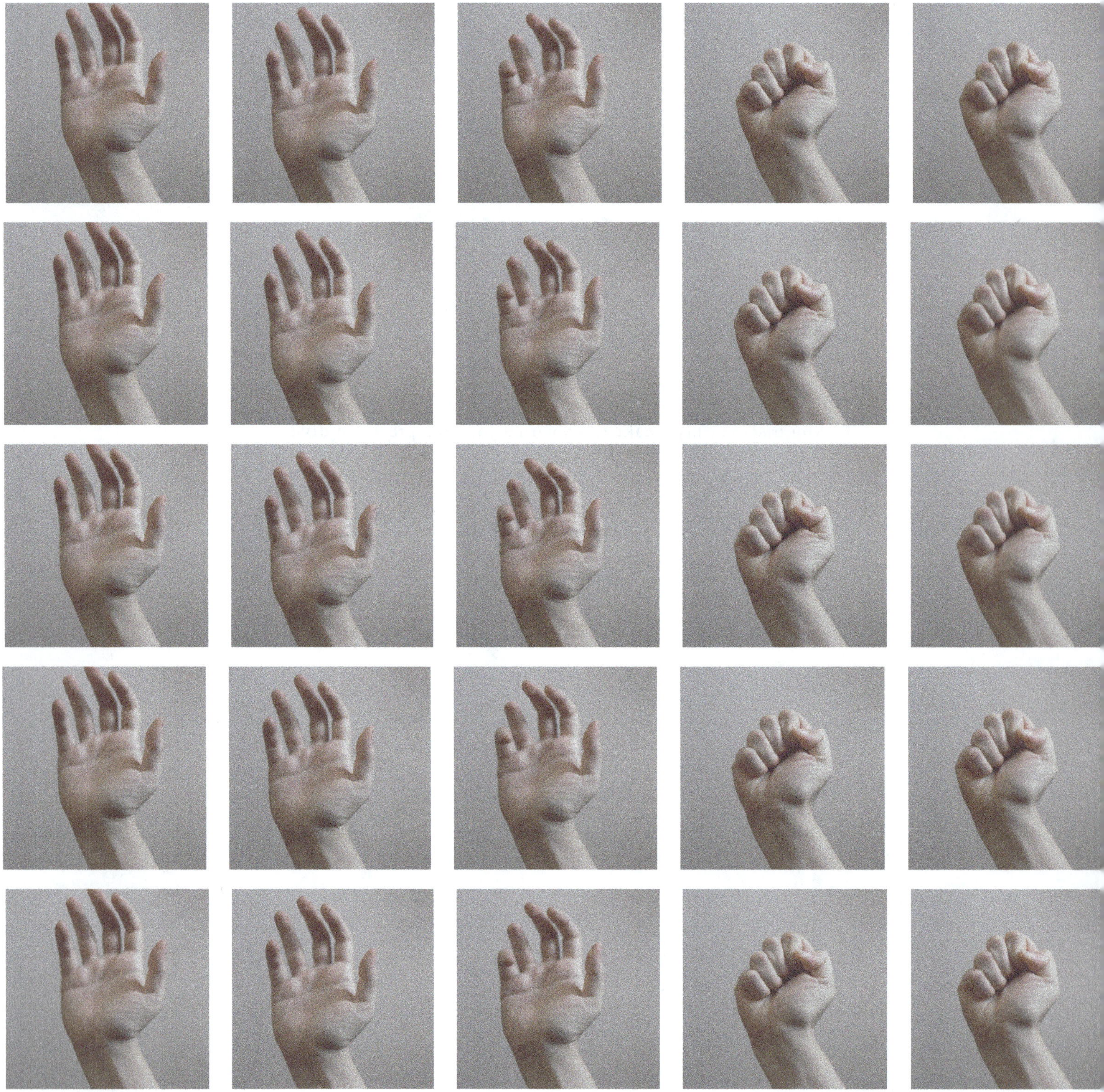

cool change

it's wet out
and I wish for a farm
of gamma-aminobutyric acid
to get that chill vibe

                                        six drinks

maybe

I've been emptying my bowels
all day / pickled fish and eggs
dreaming in monochrome
and orgasm

maybe next year we'll
paint the walls
the asbestos shed
out the back

                                        needs

some work

mostly wasps
and dog shit
my heart rate rising
as the temperature drops

it gets colder

ugh

another broken bottle
wrapped in lipstick
and the double cheeseburg bag I hid in the bin

pretend it's a fish

keep the flannelette sheets flapping in the wind
and a gimlet at my lips
a fish kiss

winter is a late night

a thick line
scrunched up oily paper
on your very worst day

pinky swear

the vermiform appendix is about the width
of my pinky finger, a narrow tube for worms.

with your hands on my abdomen, and your
thumb along my hip bone, you can't feel it

but it's there. like the finger of a glove
I once wore, warm and dark and tight like

tunnels. I will never hurt you. I will
always cut my nails before we pinky swear.

to you I vow. I swear. with this appendix
I thee wed.

pulse

the pot of lentils simmers under my
taut, wrapped wrist.
snapping snowpeas you don't talk to me.
I get stroppy when I cook
and since the dog dug up
my fledgling eggplants I've been
frowning. we try not to eat
meat these days (so many reasons)
but on afternoons like these
sometimes we should just get KFC,
give in to the humidity and grease
our fingers. see what we can
make of them. I feel now the pulse
in the bubble of the pot, your
heat behind me, this kitchen
like a dancefloor. I secrete
away a smile and stir, so tender.
turning and turning.

being asked how to cope

I am not qualified to give that kind of advice
I sleep on a boomerang pillow, wrapped around me
and I hug it for warmth

can you open your eyes under water?
perhaps that's what I'm lacking, a vision
cut slick across the lenses

washing the dishes, the sweat sticks around my
t-zone, salty like fetta, like my sinuses
I scrub and wipe and scrub

and I don't know if it's my honesty that
disarms you or the windchimes, but I'm sending
all my wishes, regardless

fear and other feelings

the

     wasp will

         just

             not fucking

                 give up

floats along our old back wall like a drone
patrolling we have cut off her access with
duct tape a mud house inside she brings
caterpillars to feed her young grasping
wriggling I think to myself what if I held
my head to the boards would I hear them
writhing they will die I watch a news report
of a dam collapsing all mud and death I do
not want to mourn my family ever it has
been three soft striped days she will not
give up I am sorry

wasp ii

a family lives
outside the front door
my bedroom window

looking up
'wasp symbolism'
on google I

learn the messages
they are trying
to send me

am I align-
ing myself
with my goals?

am I avoiding
something?
well

sipping at my soda
laptop twixt my
knees
I feel busy

dream of the seaside
in thailand
trash and rats

a guy on a scooter
opens two fingers
towards me

his tongue stuck
between. what are
you doing, girl?

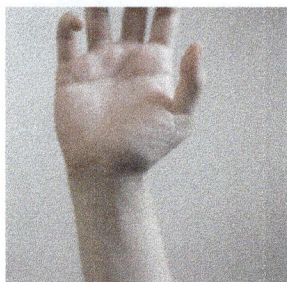

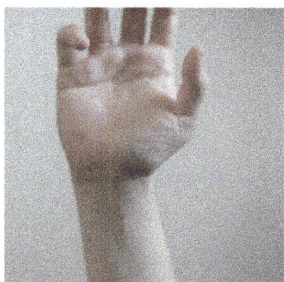

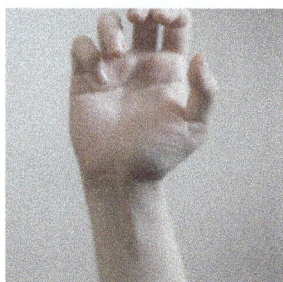

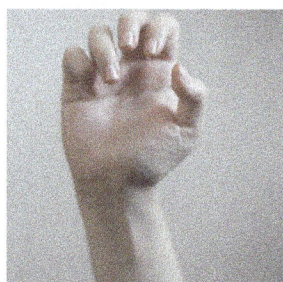

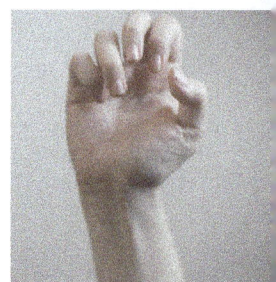

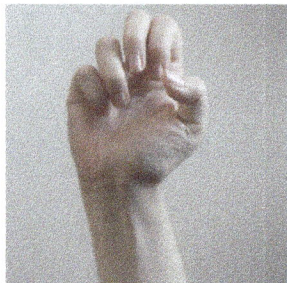

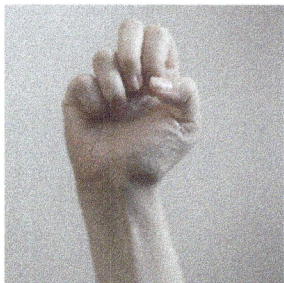

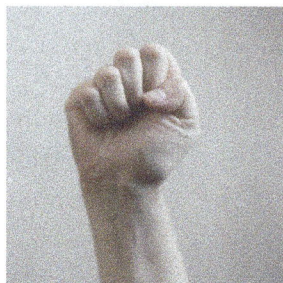

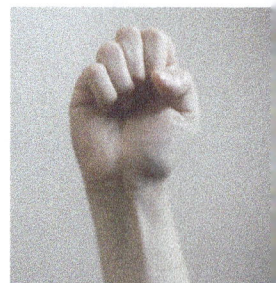

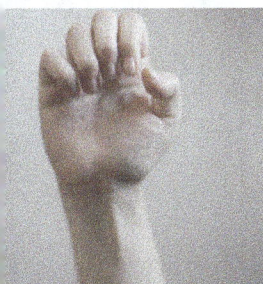

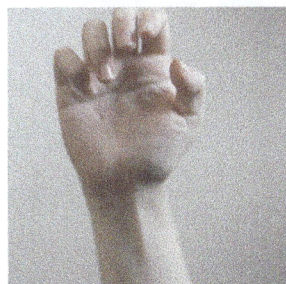

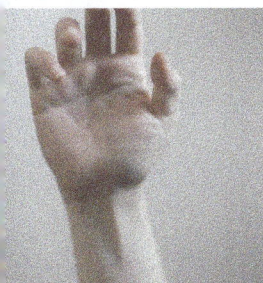

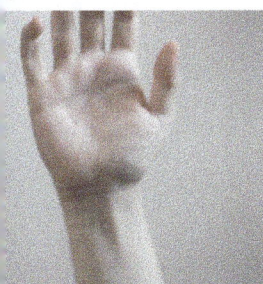

hay fever

I want to break my own wrist
into the curve of my blundstone boot

no farmer, just a subscriber
to the trade aesthetic

> [if only we knew all we needed to do
> to support drought affected Aussie farmers
> was shop at Woolworths this Saturday]

but I never could stand watching *Landline*.
I'd rather buy a bale of hay

spread it around the house
and propagate hayfever.

is this cynical? am I unfeeling?
I've watched this country die

I'm not afraid of fire
my bones are fine ground dust

a whirlybird out the car window
my breath the last clean water in the dam

bring your buffalo. put a gold coin
on its tongue. you've done your part.

scream, or, this is not a protest poem

you know things are getting
a bit chaotic
when a bullshark's driving
a fourby up the street of an after-
noon

'now that's adaptation' the fella
beside you says
out the tunnel of his cigarette

every poem is a protest poem
this man is writing a protest poem
my fingers are protest poems, my thumbs
there is no time
a raven lives in my freezer

I unbutton my shirt and out
fly a swarm of cicadas
screaming 'shiiiiiiiiiiiiiit'

and as they fly about the city
dropping shells
the key changes dramatically from
minor to major. a man turns around
and smiles, big and wide

we are eating our disasters
I am disappointed
this is not a protest poem

red eyes, silver horses

I have to leave
again
Tonight, though,
smuggling truffles out of you by the mouthful
I hold a fist inside my curve
An interrupted gesture of
goodbye
Out dirt windows black sand might be ink
brushing into mangroves
K uses an old man handkerchief
but manages to keep her cool
A few Naproxens and a lie down
I am too tired to remember how to love anyone
Naked in my hotel room I look into the bar across
the road
To see if they see these silver hairs too
But they are busy singing 'The Horses' to one another
And after the 6am gravure tones of grey, sink
down the cliffside in an elevator
Ride the free ferry, cry and cry
and cry
I don't know how to cry
The riverdrops on my cheeks play the part
At a pinch I take pictures instead

glasshouse

I want a house made of glass bricks
opaque and milky, filling rooms
with song, so as you stand
on lewis st bridge you can see it
shining, a beacon in the burbs

the blurred world seen from the inside
giving me the warm and fuzzies
golden glow in the morning
the shine of peaches at the kitchen table
juicy from every angle

I lie naked on the cold floors
singing to the bugs through
our glassy communion and laughing
at mosquitos that bust their heads
looking for blood

a blurred patchwork of trees dance the
wind's tango, the cool passing of cloud
suggests the mirror of an evening storm
and only I, fleshy and crunching,
am here, with my books and my strings

if there were a door leading to a world in focus
I might not open it, my eyes adjusted
already to the narrower apertures
of my fly house, my own kaleidoscope,
which goes to sleep with the sun

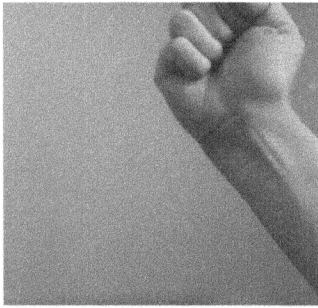

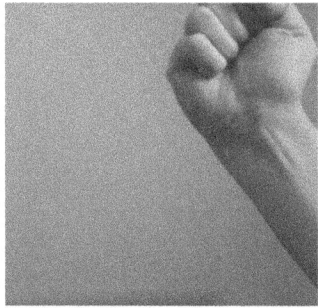

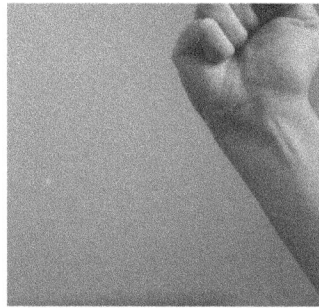

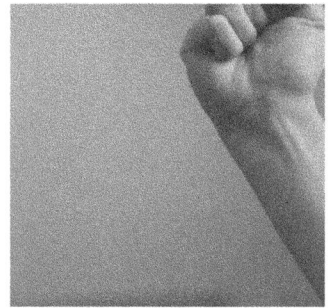

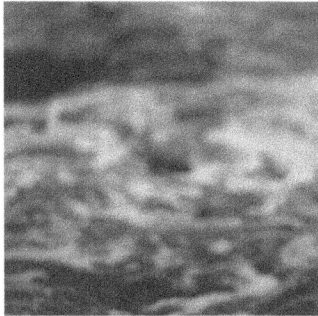

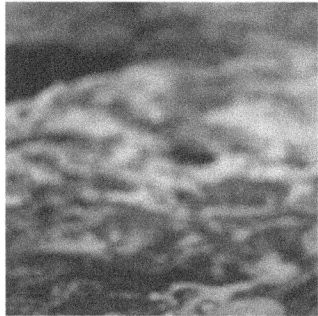

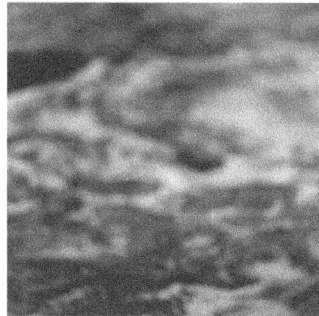

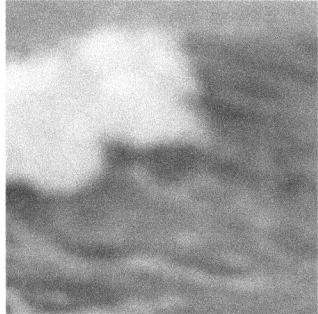

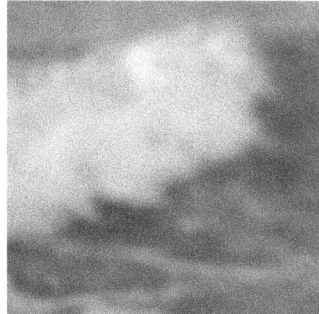

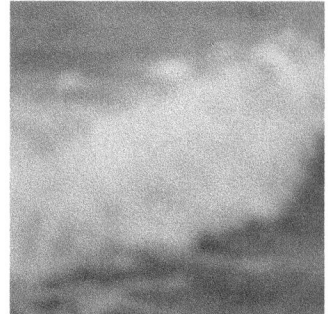

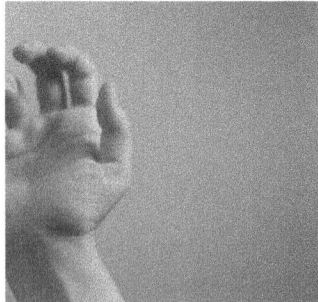

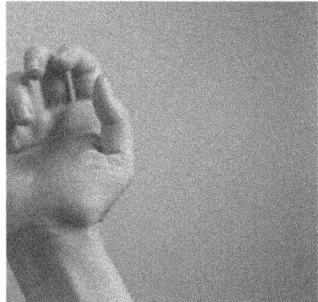

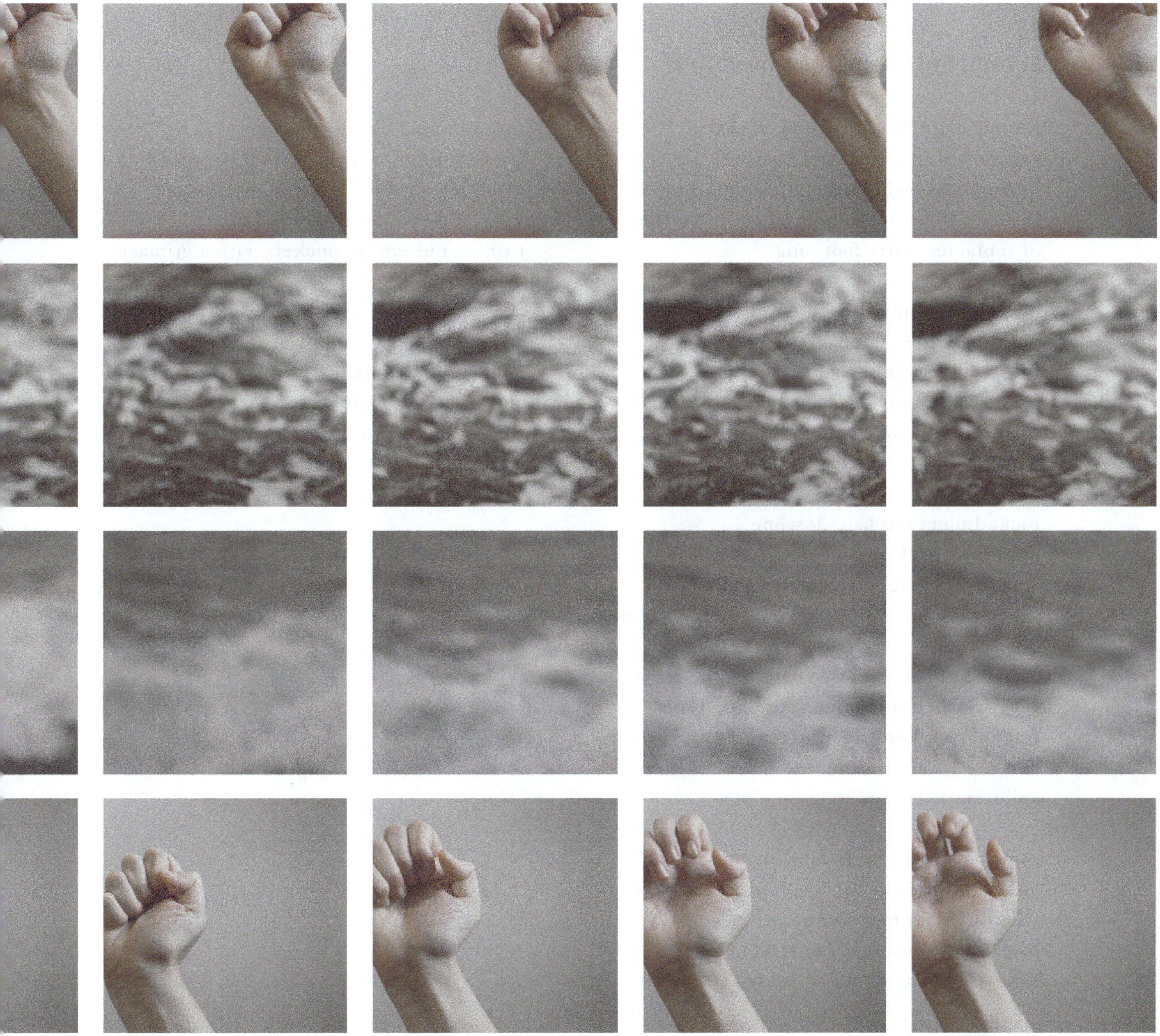

some things float, some don't

there's more debris than we think
suspended in our seas like jellies
or the bluebottle I saw drifting on the surface
the saliva on your tongue when you tell me
of tentacles thirty foot long

one night, drunk, I couldn't climb
onto the bed and fell, crashed
through the mirror that leant like a tree
against the wall and so, a sprawling corpse
on the floor, looked at spiderwebs above

then you hauled me up by my arms,
picked pieces of kaleidoscope
out of my back and pickled arse as I lay
across you, laughing, wondering how
many versions of me you could see in them

flashing about in those sharp, tactile memories
that splashed refractions out and of me
fragments taken from the frame
and it wasn't until the next day that I felt
splintered, dry and itching

there was nowhere to look for myself
and I got lost in what was left, like age 13
when I would root around in the still-warm
discarded trousers of my father
for loose change, tossing his tissues aside

those human bits and pieces
I was hungry for gold and for the smell of it
often it's hard to look him in the eye
we've taken a lot from each other
turning out empty pockets with a grimace

these days you shave my legs in the bath
soap me up as though I'm an invalid
and conjure a swirl, a storm, sometimes blood
and when we're done you say I'm smooth
like a dolphin. you love me like this.

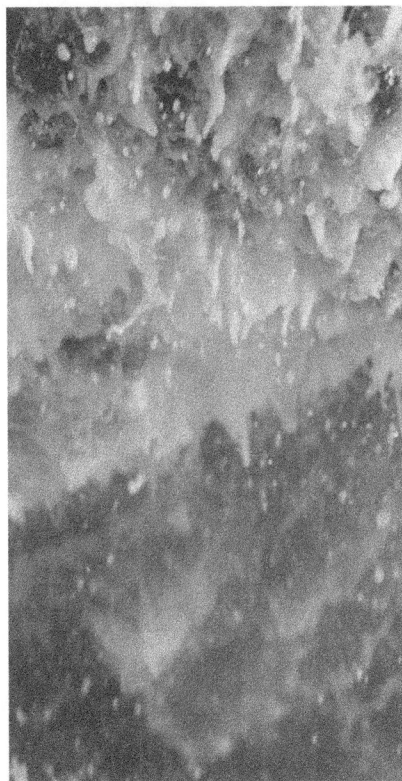

lock it in, eddie

I've been thinking of what to do
when no one will pay me to write poetry
anymore

maybe become a locksmith?
a van drives by the mayfield bowling
club and beckons

with its bolts, latches and cylinders
I inhale as the old bloke behind
moans of greenies

I want to show him a picture
of the storm a fire makes all its
own, electric

and tell him of the town in
pennsylvania where a coal blaze has
burned
for fifty years

and the trouble I've been having
breathing, anxiety or bushfire smoke
hard to say

it's a tightness of the chest just like
the air's bearing down, saying "hey
motherfuckers,

do you want me here or not?" and yes
you know I do, and I want the earth unburnt
and oceans cold

and colourful like oil on water, like your
eyes when they tell me I am going to be
okay

the rabbit's prayer

in the heaven of my god we are lobotomized
with only our skulls and their scars to remind us
of the hellish land we left behind, and dead,

like a crack along dry earth, in dust, a fissure,
an axe into a grey gum. and any pain will
fall out of it, any memory of men, of murder,

of horse-racing and banking and burnt toast
will just vanish, vanquished, like water vapor.
we will walk through a desert of upturned faces

lost in an abandonment of duty, forgotten to
boundaries and narratives, foreign to nation
and forged in the belly of a woman unknown.

with no reflection of light, we will be no colour
at all, we will form no body politic, no community,
for how to comprehend? we're brainless, quiet,

just a collection of lips and hips that pleased our
lord, our gracious pile of sticks, our generous sky
who us so blessèd took, and turned to toads.

witchcraft was our only vice, we who knew
too much and tried to purge the poison. we saw
the rabbit in the roundabout, backlit and huge

and we knew the way the traffic revolved around it,
the fear in its eyes, the shadows. we whispered spells
as we drove, round and round, never indicating.

the pull too great to resist. incant, cult, incarnate,
our carnal lines ran deep and we mined them
unsustainably. black lumps in our chest, our coal

burned into the night. the fire fell into the dishwater
of the sky and went cold. we were tired. and so,
because we slept, we lost track of the rabbit.

the traffic kept on moving, red lights in circles
could have warned us of what we already knew.
there was no way to cure the madness. we slept,

and slept, and when we woke it was worse than before.
the lights had grown to the size of planets and
the rabbit was gone. in its place, a bull, with eyes

like brake lights. so we sighed and eventually we died
and when we reached the gates we were greeted
with a scalpel and a smile. don't worry, she said,

you won't recall a thing. in the heaven of my god
we are immortalized, defeated but restored to rise
again unmolested. I do not believe in a god, at least,

but my faith in the knife is unshakeable 'til the end.

creation lament

you see the vivid in everything
I see the patina behind my eyelids
you sometimes get asthma
my heart plunks out of tune

swamping my arms through
the smoke for the first time
in four days
I open the recycling bin

and it is just an orgy
of humans, ghosts
and cool green glass bottles
all clinking together like music

and I can't tell if, in all
this, there's a line missing
a counter-melody or the alto like
some crumbled chicken stuffing

or the cork back in your bottle
that keeps it from going off
I mean a something, an extra
that's born from me

and must be kept alive
through smoke, through flood
through fear and the whole
fucking trashfire of it all

and while I suck back a
winfield and a wine I can't
help but wonder if I can't help
this, or another, or anything

resembling a future anymore
not here, not for some new creature
that doesn't want its fur all singed
or an underwater home

even though you and I
hold hands when we fall asleep
in a bad mood even
though we could make a firework

out of this furnace even though
creation could be the only thing
I'm good for - what good is creation
just to watch it gasp for life?

just to lose it? I was born
without doubt, knowing change
and floods and drought would come
and now that they're here—

I want to feel hope like a cloud
growing rain in its belly
and the rampant joy
in its wake, but my fear is unbroken

and barren, and barren, and barren

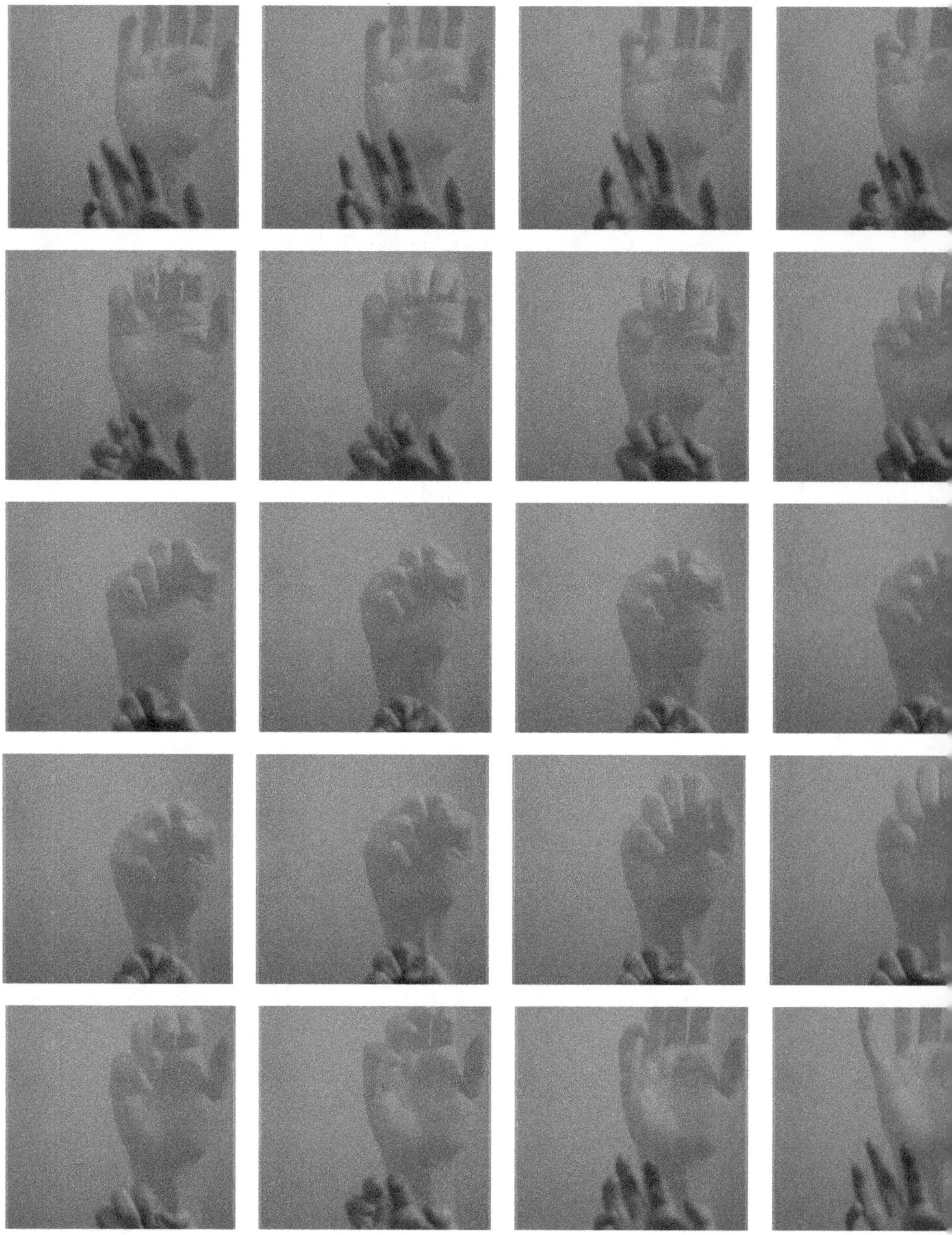

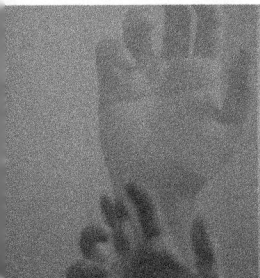

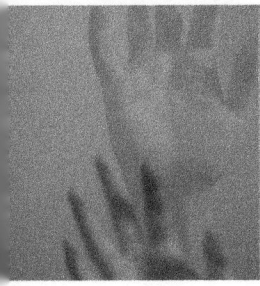

an unnamed room

in the time of coronavirus I am thinking not of love but of death
watching *Grey's Anatomy* and clenching inside when wives, husbands, children
meet the sweating crash of loss

I think all the time of what it would be like to lose you
my psychologist calls these harmful thought patterns
but I have lost the print-outs he gave me to help
instead I just scream in dream-voice repeating
as doctors elaborate the brutal details
I conjured for myself–bike accidents,
work-place injuries, several forms of cancer
that go rogue suddenly, and the more obvious

such a full-throttled scream never leaves me
even when I wake. it snuggles in for a sleep-in
and yawns out through the day, mourning you

Irregular Thought Patterns

early in the black summer fires,
two cricket teams playing not far apart
both lost a man. within minutes of each other
they clasped their chests
as toxic air gushed across the field
and died. their hearts and lungs not built to bear it.

standing at Sublime Point the sign warned
of fall hazards, an unfenced cliff edge
and I asked what it would be like to glide
down into the firelands, the ashy gullies.
just one fragment of myself floating away
into terra, below the limit, as a cloud.

I'm not afraid of death.
I am afraid of death.
I cannot judge the value of death,
or anything.
my pan-ic is sublime, goatlike,
in a world where words'r'worthless.

I'm not sure what to make of it,
or what poems are meant to do
when the heart beats so irregular like this.

ecstatic dance

for Nude on the River

murray, darling, look at me
I've lost your reflection
no narcissus in this steel gauze
and I am dancing your return
one foot, then two, the instep
a cautious depth into my own skin
I am scared of you as you kiss
my white-faced heron toes
and the sun a kiln a candle asks
to take you for its own
what pas de deux can coax
your calm return? what song
do the fish sing? I would sing it
if I knew, if you spoke to me,
murray, darling, do not
leave me like this

I have become psychologically
linked to a humpback whale

I don't know how it happened but I woke one morning tethered
across oceans, over landmass to a very large brain
approximately 4.6 kilograms—not as big as I thought it'd be
but it might have lost something in the transmission

the hook in my own head tugs as I go about my daily things
and the direction slowly moves like an orbit
the whale as he follows his trail north with the shorebirds
is a comet, an explorer before boundaries, while I wash towels

and I don't know enough about string theory to explain how
we might have been pulled together in this manner
or about quantum physics at all, come to think of it
but I know his big whale brain holds 'spindle neurons' just like mine

I imagine these as little blonde girls spinning straw into thoughts
really they are just root systems of neurons that teach us to love
and cry and talk to each other, and it seems beautiful to me
that the whale carries these too, like a songbook

in the night my 1.5kg brain writes poems with him
and we move together beneath the surface of conscious thought
I find myself waking sometimes by the sea, in wet socks
and I wonder if he sleep-swims to the shore like this

by coincidence or design we are the same age
(I can't tell you how I know this, but I do)
the same anxieties swim through our nervous systems
and along the thin silvery cord that connects us

our huge dark eyes stare into the same murky distance
we are afraid of the darkness ahead, but we move always
helped along by the comfort pulled from each other
we're strangers between realms, remote in our seas

I try to talk to him directly, forcing the connection to grow
invite him to daiquiris at the swim-up bar
but I don't know where he is exactly and I don't want him
to end up beached. that is our biggest fear

and it hovers over us daily, a dry eye crusting on sand
stranded, restless, while our body lies paralysed and useless
there is nothing satisfying about rest
we are always rolling the spindle, waving our fins in the air

I don't know why the whale pulls me along
I really don't. all I know is that I am not the frozen head
of an explorer in the Antarctic. not severed, but strung taut
and the instrument of the earth is vibrating

ghost kick

in the latest unlikely weather event we are swishing our nice black boots
through the water that bubbles up from the manhole, meanders through the park
picks up leaf litter and trips down stairs. a special little water feature.
even through these nice black blundstone boots my socks are getting wet
and I imagine all the nasty things that are in there—news reports say
absolutely No Walking, Driving, Swimming in floodwater. for fear of
snakes, sewage, bacteria, shopping trolleys. floating cars under the bridge.
I saw an image of six men drinking beers around a barrel. water up to their waists
and the first thing I thought of was: bull sharks. like the one in the front yard
at dora creek. I'm not scared of the ocean any more when the streets are
their own kind of danger. a house just floated clear away on some nice couple's
wedding day. all I have to deal with is a bundle of wet towels at my door
and the dog that refuses to go outside. a little light aquaplaning on the freeway
like a marshmallow on a hotplate. just slinking along. despite this I wake up
to the ghost kick again. something un-living in my belly. I am worried mostly
about lower things: underground carparks, basements, bunkers.
anything we could get trapped in. with the rising waters. I am afraid of being
floatless. a sinker. when our car was flooded up to its doors, we stalled on the upramp.
some bunkers aren't safe. some kicks aren't real. I don't want to go outside

skullcrushing

{{{{{{{{{{{{{{{{{{{{{(((((({{{{{{{{{{{{{{{{{{{{{{{{{{{{{{{{{{{{{{{(((((({{{{{{{{{{{{{
{{{{{{{{{{{{{{{{{{{{{{{{{{{{{{{{{{{{{(((((((({{{{{{{{{{{{{{{{{{{{{{(((((({{{{{{{{{{{{
{{{{{{{{{{I{{{{{(AM(((({{NEVER{{{{{{{{{{{QUI{ET{{{{{{{{{{{{{a{{{{
{{{xxxx{{{{{{{{{{{{{{{{{{{{{(((((((({{{{{{{{{{{{{{{{{{{{{{{{{{{{{{a{{{
{{{{{{{{{{{{{{{{{{{{{S{{{{{T{{A{{{{{T{{{{{I{{{C(((((({{{{{{a{{{
{{{{{{{{{ma{{gn{{et{s{{{{{{{{don't{{{{align{{{{{{{{{{{{{{{{{{{{a((((
{{{{{{{{(the(({{{{{C{{{{URR{{{{{{{{{{{{{{{{{{{{ENT${{{{{{{{{{{{{
{{{{{{{{{{{{{{{{{{{{{{(thecurrentsthecurrentsthecurrents){{{{{{{
{{{((((((({{{{{{{{{{{IN{{{{{H{Y{P{E{R{C{O{L(O(U(R{{{{{{{{{{{{{{{{{
{{{{allow{{{me{{{to((((({{{{{{{{{{{{{{{{{{{{{{{{{{{{(((((({{{{{{{{{
{{{{{{{{{{{{{{{{{{{{{{{{{{{{{{{understand{{{{{{{{{{{{YOU{{{{{{{{((
{{{{{{{(((((((in ways{{{{{{{{{{{{{{{{I'll{{{{{{{{{{{{{{{n{{E((v((e{{{r{{{{{{{b{{{{{
{{{{{{{{{{{A{{{ble{{{{{(((((((({2{{{{{under{{{{{{{{{{{{{{{{{{stAND
{{{{{{{{{{{{{{{{{{{{{m{{{{YSE{{{{lf{{{{{{(((((((({{{{{{{{{{{{{{{{{{{
{{((((((({{{{{{{{{{RAPIDLY{{{{{{{{{{RAPID{{{{{{{{WHITENOI$E{
{{{(((((((({{{{{{{{{{{{{{{{{
{{{(((((((((({{{{{{

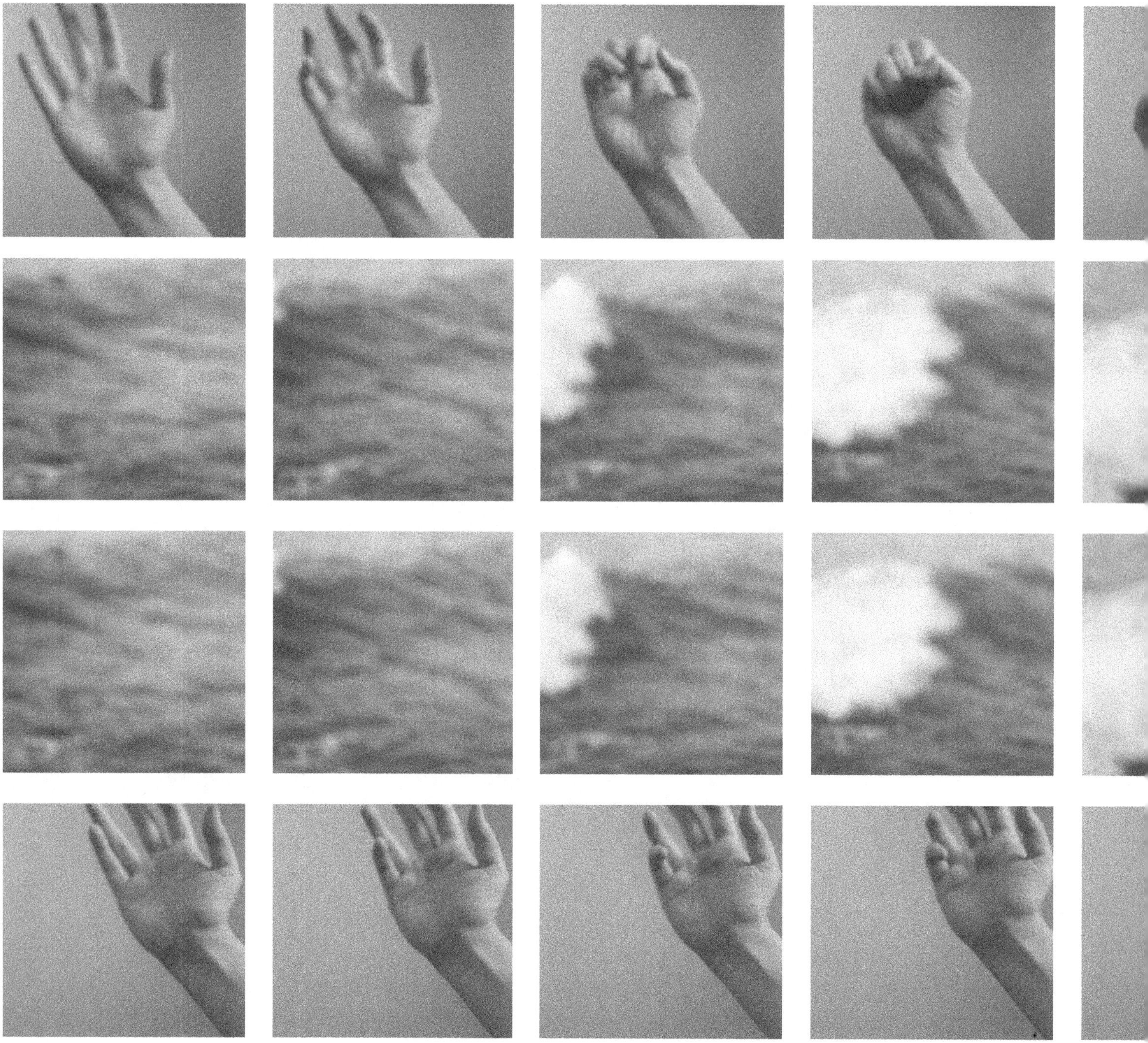

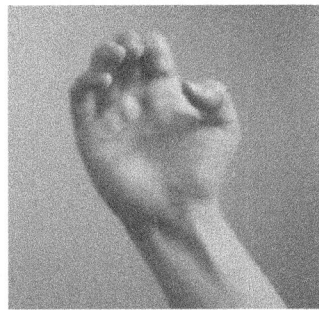

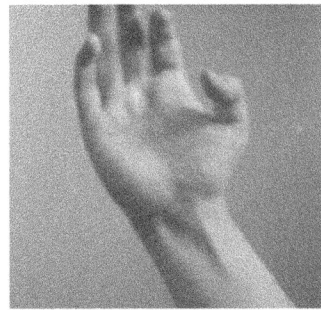

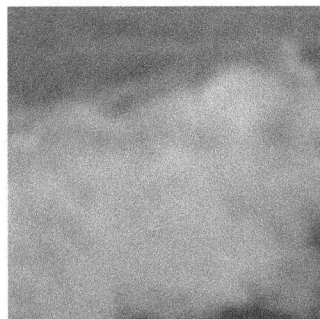

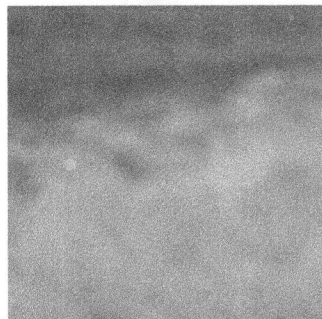

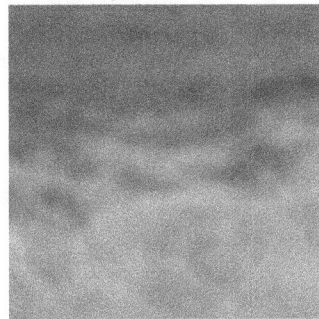

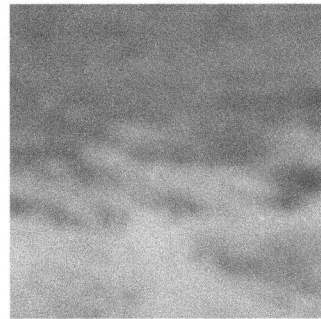

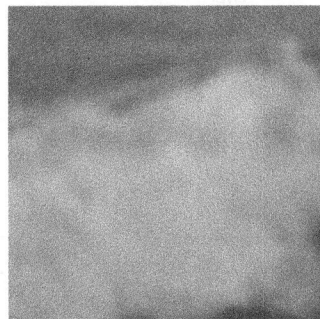

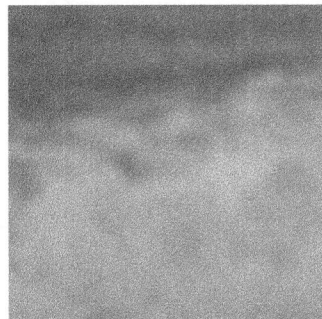

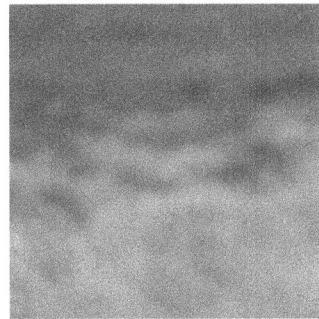

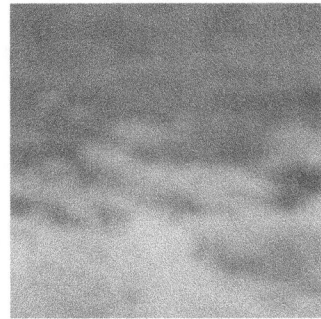

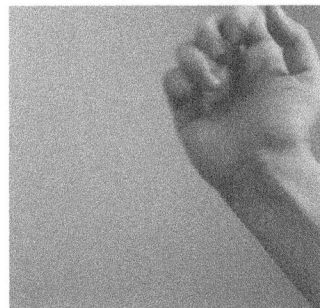

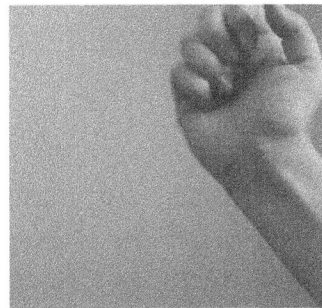

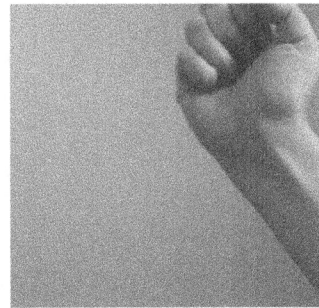

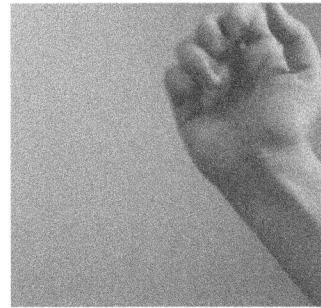

Abstracting the contract we make with ourselves

Your reflection atrophies like a Dali, like cheese dripping off toast
in this wear-nothing weather that expects something of you.
If you could imagine, if that's a thing we all can do still,
then imagine this— a house, zoom in to a boxy room, but the walls
in the house are windows, and they're all exploding, all the time.
A pulsing as they go, one by one, like a scale, only to reform
and refract each other's breaking moments, rhythmic and cyclical.
Crash scattering like a quick exhale, like the 'whoo whoo whoo'
of a woman in childbirth as she pumps the bones out of your hand,
you witness the fractious forming and unforming of anxious sublimity.

That's the difference between a pinky swear and a handshake—
it's the pressure, not the promise. Your sweat on mine, the sticky
date our fingerprints make in this psychosomatic social contract,
you hear the tiny tinkling screams of broken glass as it tightens.
In a stinking haze you hook and squeeze for pleasure, for security, for
a second outside of yourself, and find an empty room.

hold on

anxiety, like poetry, is the beat
that you feel in your wrist
after the heart throbs
and you try not to lose it

annexiety

anxiety is the millennial condition, says a clickbait article I
think I read somewhere; as for my own tangles, well,
there are some parties you just shouldn't go to.
I'm one gnarled shoot of a gnarly nervous system,

jacked up on caffeine-free cokes and celery and
clenching my teeth at that cunt of a waiter, who probably
had a panic attack five minutes ago. this basically
makes us sisters. 'you aren't lazy, you're just terrified'

is the latest feel-good production of the meme machine, but
I can tell you right now, I'm definitively both - don't pretend
they're mutually exclusive. I can drop a potato chip
down the sleeve of my knitted jumper while I fear for

all our futures, eye the vacuum off for months feeling petrified
of filling one. but what's a bit of dust floating around? at night
I try to dream of Putin, just to see what he'd be like,
shirtless, playing piano; I sprawl naked on his lounge

stringing cheese between my fingers and feeling the soft-
ness of what's probably bear pelt tucked up under my arse.
I tell him he can sanction and annex whatever he likes,
if he promises not to meddle in my domestic affairs and

we watch porn together, tapes of Trump pissing on women,
he tells me his fantasies and I tell him mine, and when I try
to fuck him from behind he gets antsy, grunts out a veto,
something about NATO and the security of his borders and

I get bored again, make a smoothie and sit cross-legged on
my deck watching bats. things like, do you think Princess Diana
liked pineapple on her pizza? not a metaphor, but I'd be interested
either way. my earrings shake in the air like icicles in an earthquake.

apologies for ~~explanation towards~~ being ~~a poet~~ this person

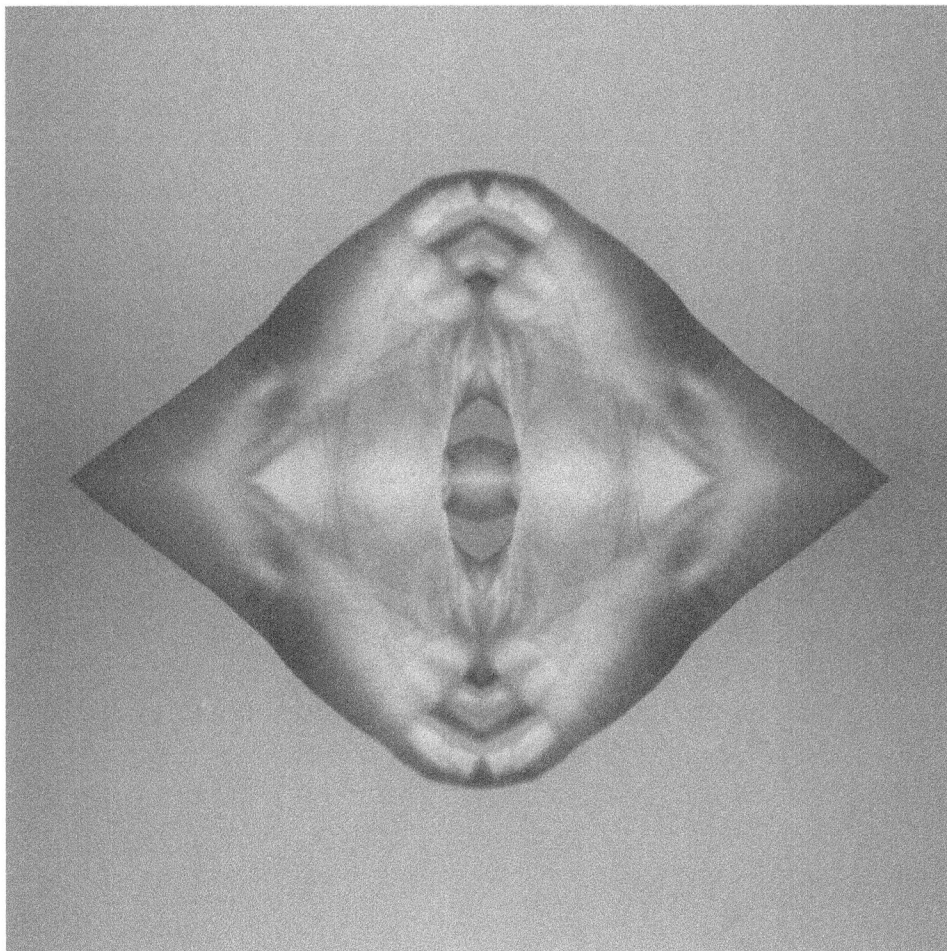

continental drift (or flight shame)

the shape of the land's edge is undemocratic
moving in ways we haven't allowed for, shifting

                              I take photos
                        on   my   phone
                        out   the   window
                        of   the   harbour
                        pulling away, the
                        slow   insistence,
                        the   imperceptible
                        drifting of waves
                        from   above

I have paid $2.88 to offset my carbon load
and feel the hum of the engine's approval

                    snow   on
                    the   tops   of
                    these   mountains
                    like a bald spot
                    asking   the   sky
                    not to notice it
                    and   a   river
                    that hummed once
                        now   shush

and on Monday I will fly again, and again
count the credits, my frequent flyer points

    on my screen,
through   this
window, it is even
more   beautiful
than   reality
a   moving   picture
a   rolling   reel
interrupted   by
coal   mines

will you forgive me? I cannot sail like greta
and my wings have not grown in as promised

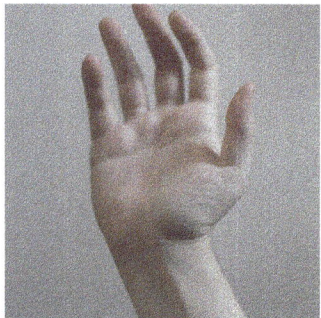

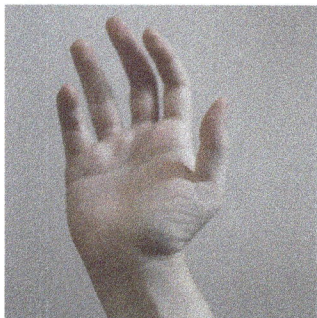

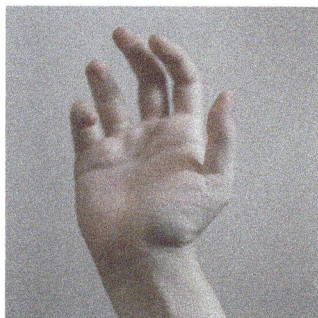

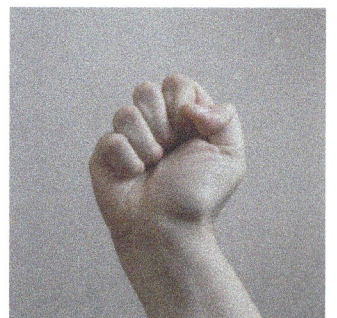

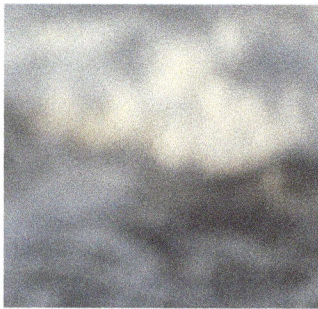

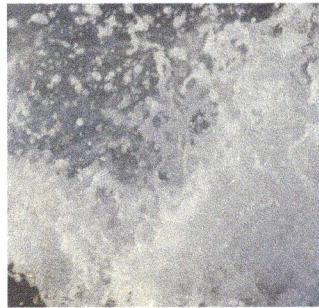

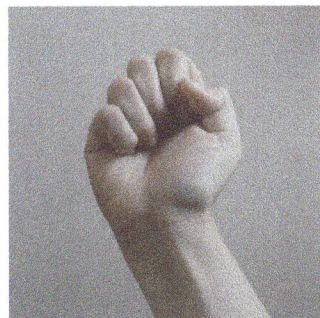

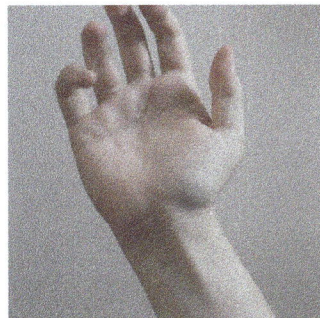

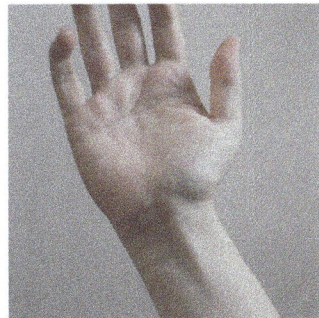

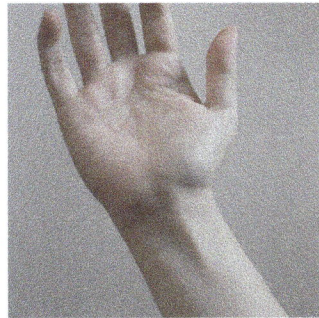

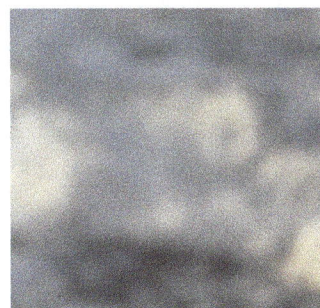

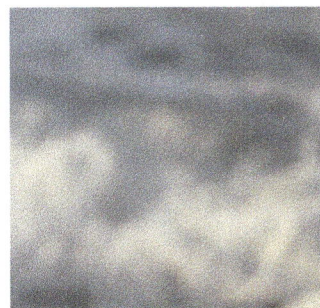

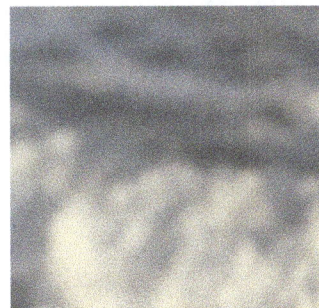

blank slates

I can't write funny poems anymore
I am no longer charming
no wry remarks on *Masterchef* Season 12
pasta is just pasta
and I am just on the couch
again, shutters closed

and I can only write lines like:
mirrors are blank in the absence of light
and
what if I never went outside again
and you look at me like "oh no"
like you don't know where to pull me from

singing karaoke for trump at an
australian xmas bbq

I am wearing every piece of clothing I can find
inc. scarves, hats, gloves, sarongs, multi-pack bonds singlets
to disguise my shape and bodily nuances
this is the first step
our nephews are playing cricket with a plastic bat
yelling 'howzat' and the more contemporary 'nice garry'
one uncle is sizzling up some rump steak and chicken
little parcels of fish in foil
snapping his tongs like turtles in a bad mood
I am sweating now
and I step up to the mic
begin with a swingin' number
trumpets, bit sexy, with some scat
then cher's [redacted]
as I autotune myself, tweaking the levels
plagiarise some other famous line
as a kind of drag, my fancy wig
and when I get to that final song
my swan song, squash song, strumpet song
the backyard goes quiet
crickets stop
a kid is mid munch on an orange

and our special guest, flown in
from the white house, begins to blossom
with rage as I sing vitamin c's [redacted]
just like at my own graduation
and a generation of others, holding hands
and crying as we wave each other out of our youth
in that psychotic hyper saturation
of a decade
I am not one to hold a grudge
and I like to say goodbye
but as he kicks over our christmas ornaments
and overturns the mini fridge
to such an innocuous tune
I find myself encouraging rebellion
inciting cricket bats, glassings,
throwing my gloves and even the umpire
is letting loose now
we're in it together
I stand on the roof and screech like a madwoman
calling lightning from the heavens
or santa on his sleigh to take the
man away

crown shy

I want my family the way oceans want shores
tidal forces advancing and repelling

the way that tree crowns edge away from one another
making maps in the canopy

nations nestled just so, some breathing room
in generational diplomacy

and when the wind blows it's camera shake
the lines blur, borders break

leaves like hands reach out
and touch their second skin

their kinfolk, their ocean grasses
before collecting themselves

retreating, shy and tired
to take their places

in a portrait pulled apart
an unmade jigsaw on the coffee table

we take a photo and tell each other we'll remember
to try again next year

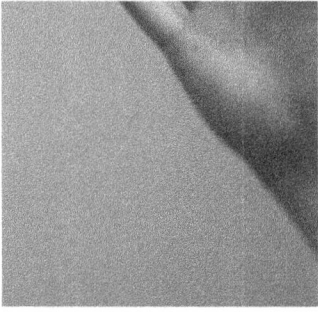

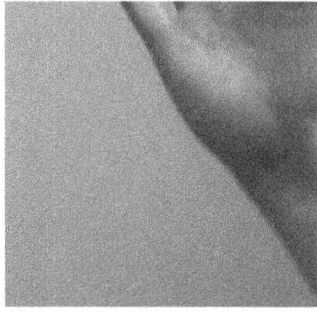

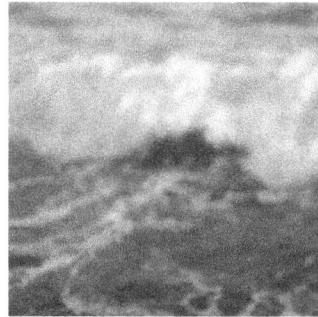

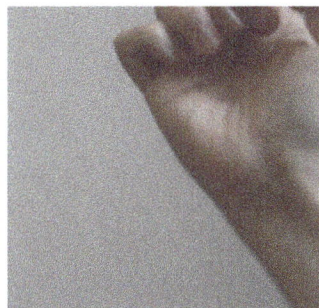

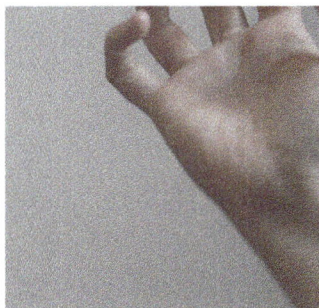

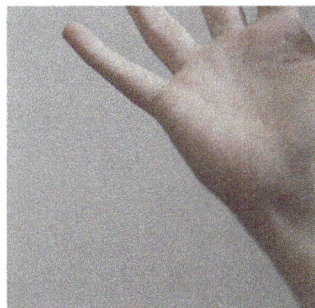

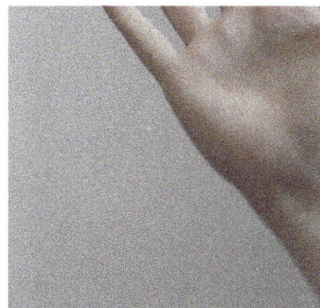

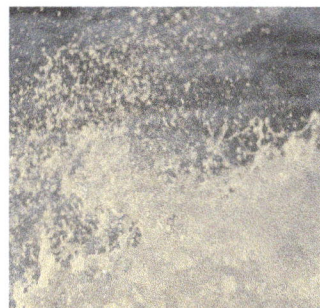

a peregrine falcon

hovers	above
this grand	canyon
wings attempt	a vastness
contextually	equal to such an
almighty	chasm, if a ratio
of one free	bird : eternity,
I see from his	eyes as though
I am he for a	second, lord of air
pockets and thermal	energy, sweep down
at the insistence of	movement on cliff face
and touch the only true	history with the tips of
my flight feathers, feel	the aching resonance of
eons and eons and eons	of rivers and rivers and rivers
clutching in towards the	earth as I gain speed, you see
me like water through air	you perch up there like a toy bird
drinking tins of beer you	trace the angles of this depression
with your retinas to recall	you take the measure of distance
you will remember when	you lie awake at night you will see
the forever of the world in	catch the light of my eyes in its glow
the colorado,	

cell safety

when you rub your eyes
deep with long fingernails
you feel the push and pull
of the rubbing tides
these slippery, wet pools
inside your skull, you rub
and rub like you are trying
to burst an egg yolk
which is a single cell, you heard,
just a bobbing, lonely mass

your eye cells multiply
iris on iris on iris
probing in on each other
when you rub the reflections run
into the next frame
like unfocused binoculars
looking out to sea, twin boats
on the water, twin whales
a gaze that multiplies the world
and unveils the mirror

now there are hundreds of whales
waiting their turn to be real
each believing it more than the next
and, sparkling, each drop of spray
holds a whale eye perfectly framed
perfectly forced into forever
sometimes it helps you
to forget these small infinities
return to the yolk and
rub her walled cell's solitude

gr-attitude

it's been pissing down for days

ants in my jaffle iron
sad cockroach in the third drawer down
slippery green deck

everyone hiding or
making themselves impervious

today, bright flocks of
sulphur-crested cockatoos
on ceramic blue

bees around the washing line
towels waving them in

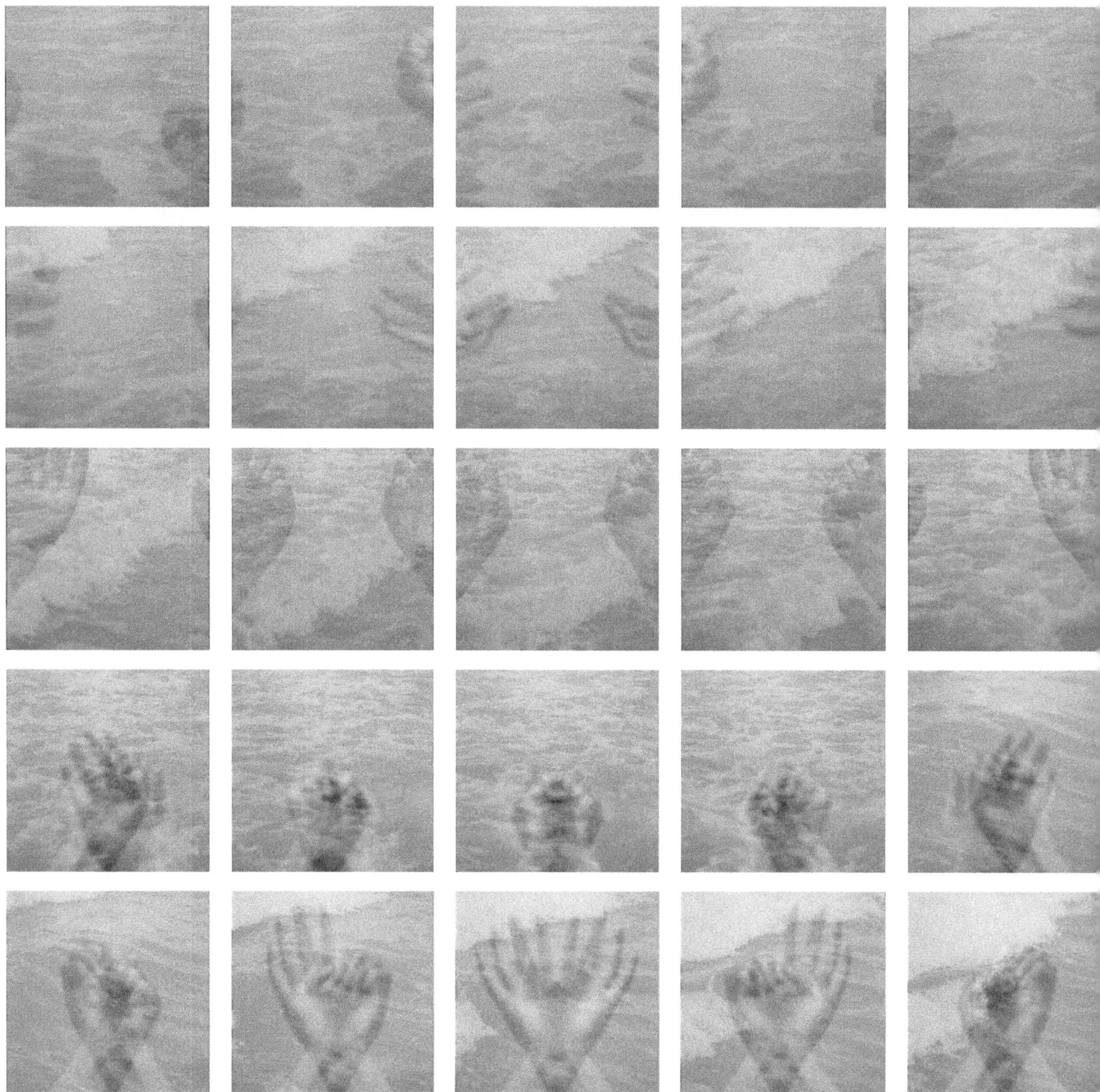

rose meditation

on the inhale, a stalk poles up, a bud forms
on the exhale, the flower blooms then dies

watching surfers and swinging my legs about

at newy beach. swimmers in my tiny pink bag, but it's windy and
there's rain over the cargo ships. moving rapidly. I pull the band
of my jeans up and sit with the green ants. arcade fire's *the suburbs*
playing. I'm very 2010-dy. boyo out with his board turns back to see
if I'm watching. the anxiety makes it hard. stomach knots on sand-
banks. but I'm feeling good today, swinging my legs about, scratching
my newly painted nails on the rocks and not getting mad when some
kids make me move. I'll just get back up? things are easy? not even
fussed about the rejection email I got this morning. just swinging
my legs about. watching surfers. with the wind coming. dark clouds.
feeling good. playing out my own little poem.

Acknowledgements

Poems in this collection have appeared in *Best of Australian Poems Vol. 1, The Suburban Review, Baby Teeth Journal, Cordite Poetry Review, Overland Literary Journal, Mascara Literary Review, Minarets, StylusLit, Tell Me Like You Mean It Vol. 3, Revue Post,* and Red Room Poetry's *Writing Water*. 'I have become psychologically linked to a humpback whale' was shortlisted for the Newcastle Poetry Prize and published in the accompanying anthology.

The collection was written, for the most part, on unceded Awabakal and Worimi land.

Many thanks to Ed and David at Puncher & Wattmann for supporting my poetry as it grows and develops. This collection began as a creative manuscript for a Doctorate of Philosophy at the University of Newcastle, supported by an Australian Government Research Training Program (RTP) Scholarship. Particular thanks go to Keri Glastonbury for encouraging me to write poems in the first place, and for seeing this through with patience and trust. To my additional PhD supervisors Erin McCarthy and Deidre Brollo, many thanks for your insights, recommendations and ideas, which shaped my attitude towards the whole experience.

I must also acknowledge the mental health services available in this flawed country, which allowed me to complete *handshake* without giving in to the panic completely.

Finally, my eternal gratitude to my family and husband, who gave me all the praise and support I demanded, and more.

www.ingramcontent.com/pod-product-compliance
Lightning Source LLC
Chambersburg PA
CBHW081340090426
42737CB00017B/3226